THE
QUEEN'S
WAY

A Celebration of Biblical
Discipleship in Public Life

MARK GREENE

The London Institute for Contemporary Christianity
St Peters Church Vere Street
licc.org.uk
hello@licc.org.uk
020 7399 9555

First published 2022.

British Library Cataloguing-in-Publication Data

A catalogue record for this book is available from the British Library.

ISBN: 978-1-8384535-1-0

Cover Illustration and Typeset in Great Britain by Michael Ridley

Print coordinated in Great Britain by Haynes Mear

With great gratitude to
Her Majesty Queen Elizabeth II
for her example, and great
gratitude to God for her.

May 2022

'...the Son of Man did not come to
be served, but to serve, and to give
his life as a ransom for many.'

Matthew 20:28

WHAT'S
HER
SECRET?

Do anything really well in almost any sphere of life – run a business, run a marathon, run a country – and pretty soon people want to know your secret.

What motivated you? Where did you get your inspiration and stamina? What were your guiding principles?

Her Majesty The Queen has rightly been globally praised for doing an outstanding job since she came to the throne at the age of 25. And for 70 years she's done her work as Queen, Head of the Commonwealth, and Supreme Governor of the Church of England with amazing diligence, great grace, astute intelligence, deep humility, and tremendous effectiveness.

Where does all that come from – the clarity of vision, the stamina, the steadfastness in duty and care? What has shaped and sustained this remarkable stateswoman? While we know very little about what she thinks about a whole host of issues, she has been extraordinarily clear about where her guiding principles come from – though the majority of her biographers have rarely paid serious attention to her words.

Her answer can be summed up in one word: Jesus.

It is, as she testifies, Jesus' teaching that has shaped her, Jesus' example that has inspired her, and Jesus' power that has enabled her to do the job God called her to do.

We can see it in her actions. The fruit of the Spirit has been rich in her: love, joy, peace, patience, kindness, goodness, faithfulness, gentleness, and self-control. And we hear it in her words. She has repeatedly communicated the reality of her own faith in Christ and the difference he has made to her life in a clear and winsome way, most notably in her Christmas addresses.

This essay doesn't reprise the key events of Her Majesty's reign – there's much on that in my book *The Servant Queen and the King She Serves*. Rather, it looks more deeply at the character of the Queen's faith: its biblical roots, and her understanding of Jesus and his priorities. And it explores how those have shaped her as a disciple, her vision for her role as sovereign, her vision for the nations and their citizens, and her vision for the Commonwealth.

The primary sources for these reflections are her Christmas addresses, precisely because she writes them herself, sometimes seeking suggestions from people close to her – her private secretary, or, in the past, Prince Philip. Of course, her broadcasts are not sermons or theological treatises. They are short (around 750 words), they cover a range of topics, and their starting point is Christmas, not Easter or Pentecost. Nevertheless, when combined these 'epistles to the nations' offer us a radical, attractive, and distinctively biblical vision for what it means to be a whole-life disciple of Jesus day by day in God's world.

'For me, the life of Jesus Christ, the Prince of Peace... is an inspiration and an anchor in my life. A role-model of reconciliation and forgiveness, he stretched out his hands in love, acceptance, and healing. Christ's example has taught me to seek to respect and value all people of whatever faith or none.'

Elizabeth ll
Christmas Address 2014

CHRIST
HER
COMPASS

Almost every time the Queen speaks about her faith she relates it directly to Jesus. And she is effusive in her appreciation. He is 'the bedrock of my faith' (2014), 'an inspiration and an anchor in my life' (2014), and 'the compelling example' (1978). 'The teachings of Christ have served as my inner light' (2020).

The biblical resonances with these words are not hard to find. The God who is a rock (1 Samuel 2:2), 'this hope that we have as an anchor' (Hebrews 6:19), the Christ who we are to imitate (Ephesians 5:1-2), the Son who is the light of the world (John 1:4). But there is a certain originality in the language. 'Rock' may be a common metaphor for Christ, but 'bedrock' isn't. 'Anchor' in Hebrews refers to the good news as a whole but the Queen applies it to Jesus himself. Christ as our 'example' may be a well-worn concept, but the adjective 'compelling' suggests an intensity of personal engagement. Good teaching as a 'light' is a familiar idea (Psalm 119:105), but 'my inner light' points to an intimacy with Christ, to an experience of his indwelling, reminiscent of both of Christ's words 'You are in me, and I am in you' (John 14:20) and of the Spirit who is in Christ's followers (John 4:14) who guides and encourages (John 14:26). Jesus is no mere idea, not a remote figure in another dimension of reality but a person she relates to.

Furthermore, there is a richness of imagination in her writing. Here's the poetic picture she paints of Bethlehem in 1954: 'Life in such a place might have been uneventful. But the Light, kindled in Bethlehem and then streaming from the cottage window in Nazareth, has illumined the world for two thousand years. It is in the glow of that bright beam that I wish you all a blessed Christmas and a happy New Year!' The beam is 'bright' and the faith she commends is 'joyful' (2013).

She sees in Christ not only a teacher who 'revealed to us the truth in his teaching', but someone who 'lived by what he believed and gave us the strength to do the same.' His actions match his words and 'on the cross, he showed the supreme example of

'For me, the teachings
of Christ and my own
**personal accountability
before God** provide a
framework in which
I try to lead my life.
I, like so many of you,
have drawn great
comfort in difficult
times from Christ's
words and example.'

Elizabeth II
Christmas Address 2000

physical and moral courage' (1981). The occasion for the Queen's address may be Christmas, but the reason for celebrating Jesus' birth is the significance of his life and death. As she put it, 'That sacrifice was the dawn of Christianity, and this is why at Christmas time we are inspired by the example of Christ as we celebrate his birth' (1981).

Indeed, as the years have gone by, the Queen has focused more explicitly on how Christ offers hope. It is not just that he is the light of the world but that the light points to particular ways of living. In 1972, as the conflict in Northern Ireland continued to maim and kill, she spoke clearly about her own yearning and hope: 'Christ taught love and charity and that we should show humanity and compassion at all times and in all situations.'

She was under no illusion as to the scale of the challenges, challenges that she encouraged people to resolve by turning to God in prayer and to Christ for guidance. At the end of the address, recognising that resolving the conflict would take something beyond ourselves, she called on people not only to pray but to pray *with her* and look to Christ's wisdom:

> *'I ask you all to join me in praying that the hearts and minds of everyone in that troubled Province may be touched with the spirit of Christmas and the message of brotherhood, peace, and goodwill. May*

> tolerance and understanding release the people from terror and put gladness in the place of fear. I leave with you the old message, "On earth peace; goodwill toward men". No one has ever offered a better formula and I hope that its simple truth may yet take hold of the imagination of all mankind.'

For Elizabeth, Christ's 'formula' works in the real world. Indeed, one of the things she admires about Christ's teaching is that it is practical. Faith in him should lead to works for him, works that have a particular selfless character.

Christ as servant lies at the heart of it all:

> 'This is the time of year when we remember that God sent his only son "to serve, not to be served". He restored love and service to the centre of our lives in the person of Jesus Christ.' (2012)

The Queen is quoting Jesus' words from Mark 10:45: 'For even the Son of Man did not come to be served, but to serve, and to give his life as a ransom for many.' Here the inclusion of 'love' in the sentence is telling. Her understanding of service is not limited to some dour, clenched-teeth sense of duty, but is rooted in compassion. Vitally, for her, service is not some leisure-time activity, not expressed only in volunteering to help out in a homeless shelter or take a meal to a neighbour, though she affirms all such activities. Rather, it is 'central'. It is the fountain from which all else flows.

It is the very posture of her life, and it derives from her understanding not only of Jesus' own character but of his mission – Christ is seeking to form people who are selfless, other-oriented, servant-hearted – whatever their status, job, or role.

The concept of servant leadership has been much explored in management and leadership circles since 1970, when Robert Greenleaf began to popularise it. But it is rare indeed to see anyone who has lived it out as richly and consistently as the Queen, for so long. And rare, too, to find a public figure who so consciously models her leadership on Christ's pattern (Philippians 2:6-8).

For her, service and love are bound together. Service should lead to taking initiative to love one's neighbour, and neighbour-love should be shaped by selfless service rather than self-interest. And that has been the keynote of her reign. It is what she highlights in Christ, what she calls others to, and what she aspires to herself: 'I declare before you all that my whole life, whether it be long or short, shall be devoted to your service.' That's the promise she made to the nation and Commonwealth on her 21st birthday. Seventy-four years later she returned to that theme in her short Platinum Jubilee letter, opening her final paragraph with these words:

'And so, as I look forward to continuing to serve you with all my heart[...]'

And then she ended the letter with the most concise of self-descriptions:

'Your Servant, Elizabeth R.'

It is an example to any leader. And any follower.

'In difficult times we may be tempted to find excuses for self-indulgence and to wash our hands of responsibility. Christmas stands for the opposite... we need to go out and look for opportunities to help those less fortunate than ourselves, even if that service demands sacrifice.'

Elizabeth II
Christmas Address 1980

A
VISION
FOR THE
NATION

As we've seen, the Queen's understanding of her role is deeply shaped by the Jesus of the Bible. It's not surprising, then, that her vision for the nation and her vision for her people find their roots in a biblical understanding of national purpose and civic service.

In terms of her own role, the Queen was never under any kind of illusions about the extent of her own power. In 1956, she said:

> *'I cannot lead you into battle, I do not give you laws or administer justice, but I can do something else. I can give you my heart and my devotion to these old islands and to all the people of our brotherhood*

of nations. I believe in our qualities and in our strength. I believe that together we can set an example to the world which will encourage upright people everywhere...'

In the context of Britain's imperial past, this is a remarkable vision. It is not a vision of military superiority, economic dominance, ideological hegemony, creative brilliance, or sporting excellence, but of moral example. It is a vision designed not to inspire envy or fear but to encourage generosity, justice, kindness, and 'uprightness'. It is made all the more remarkable by the historical context. She was, after all, the granddaughter of a king who had ruled over a quarter of the planet. The British government still saw itself as a significant player on the world stage, and over 70 territories were under its colonial rule. Yet there is not a smidgen of nostalgia for the empire, not a whiff of the triumphalist bluster about Britain being a 'world beater' that characterises current political rhetoric. For Elizabeth, what has mattered most is to be an encouragement to 'upright' people.

The word 'upright' feels old-fashioned, but even today it speaks of integrity, honesty, and commitment to principle. In the sense of 'moral integrity', it appears 93 times in the King James Bible, the version that the Queen reads. There, the word 'upright' is used to translate two key words in the original Hebrew – one meaning 'straight' or 'right', the other meaning 'perfect in moral character'. Of course, back in the 1950s 'upright' might well have been in general use, but coming from the mouth of a Queen who read the Bible every day as a child, reads it almost every day as an adult, and attends a church service almost every week, it is extremely likely that the biblical connection was in her mind.

This desire that post-Imperial Britain would be a positive moral example to others has a strong resonance with the vision that the people of Israel were given by God: that they would be 'a light unto the nations' (Isaiah 42:6). The biblical nation of Israel was relatively small in area and small in population. And it was not marked out for regional or global domination. Rather, it was intended that their devotion to God and his ways, and their testimony to his mighty deeds, would serve as a powerful witness and blessing to surrounding countries.

The Queen's focus was similar: Britain would be famous for its 'uprightness'.

Not surprisingly, such a vision leads inevitably to a particular understanding of the qualities that go into being a good citizen.

The Queen's vision for citizenship is shaped by two main ideas – service and neighbour-love. Both are at the heart of her own life and Christian living, but you don't have to be a Christian to think that they're important. Neither are necessarily distinctively Christian. But the Queen's presentation of them is.

She roots her understanding of these two concepts in the life and teaching of Christ. It's important to note that she didn't need to do that. After all, an appeal to selfless service and generous neighbourliness is hardly controversial, even if it is rarer than we would like. Again and again, however, often quoting the Bible, she makes it clear that Christ's life and teaching shape her vision of what service and neighbour-love look like and what it takes to live them out.

It is because Christ is 'the Prince of Peace' (Isaiah 9:6) that we should 'work to heal old wounds and to abandon prejudice and suspicion' (1984).

It is because of Christ's example that we are given courage to live in line with the principles he teaches:

> 'Our Christian faith helps us to sustain those convictions. Christ not only revealed to us the truth in his teachings. He lived by what he believed and gave us the strength to try to do the same – and, finally, on the cross, he showed the supreme example of physical and moral courage.' (1990)

It is because the 'inheritance of the earth which Christ promised,' was 'not to the strong, but to

Christmas speeches
where the Queen
mentions looking
out for neighbours or
disadvantaged people.

1950s	○○○●●○●○
1960s	○●●●●●●○●●
1970s	○●●●●●○○○●
1980s	●●●●○○○●○●
1990s	○○●●●○●●●●
2000s	●●●●●●○●●●
2010s	●●●●●●●●●●
2020s	●●

the meek' (1990), referring to Matthew 5:5, that she affirms those who do not respond to 'the loud voice and a strong arm' with violence and vitriol, but with gentleness.

It is because Christ said, 'Blessed are the peacemakers' (Matthew 5:9) that she affirmed ordinary people pursuing peace in troubled lands – particularly 'those who are hardly aware of what they do' (1995).

Similarly, the Queen frequently expresses her concern for the grieving and for those 'on the edge of society' – the lonely, the hungry, the poor, people who 'feel cut off and disadvantaged', for whom 'the world can seem a distant and hostile place' (2007). Her compassion is clear. Again, you don't have to be a Christian to do that, but the Queen has made it clear that her concern springs from Christian teaching 'to love their neighbours, having compassion and concern, and being ready to undertake charity and voluntary work to ease the burden of deprivation and disadvantage' (2009).

It's rare to hear a leader who is not ordained in a particular faith community being so clear about the source of their ideas and so keen to make that source clear to others.

Her focus on Christ also expresses itself in the way she makes explicit connections between the challenging circumstances people face today and Christ's life – citing, for example, the adverse circumstances of his birth (1956), the displacement and persecution he suffered (2015), or the rejection he experienced (2016). This is in line with the Bible's pervasive concern for the poor and the marginalised (Deuteronomy 15:11; 24:10-12; Amos 8:4-14), and also with the biblical portrait of Jesus as the God who understands our suffering because he too suffered (Hebrews 2:10).

This sensitivity to the perennial challenges of life is reinforced by the astute way the Queen acknowledges, as the biblical texts do, the particular challenges of the moment. So, in 1960, with the growing threat of nuclear war between the USA and the USSR, she said with typical understatement, 'By no stretch of the imagination can 1960 be described as a happy or successful year for mankind...' She then went on to directly address the sense of powerlessness and hopelessness that people felt, offering an antidote in the form of the 'everyday behaviours' through which anyone can contribute to positive change.

For her, selflessness is the key. Several times she's used the parable of the Good Samaritan to highlight some particular aspect of what loving your neighbour might look like in everyday life. In 2004, she focused on race. She pointed out that the victim of the mugging in the parable was 'ignored by his own countrymen' but helped by a foreigner – 'and a despised foreigner at that'. The implication is clear: everyone is our neighbour, no matter what race, creed, or colour. The need to look after another human being is far more important than any cultural or religious difference. Importantly, for her, the litmus test is not merely that people 'acknowledge and respect' 'other cultures and religions' but how 'those from different backgrounds behave towards each other in everyday life.'

Again, we see a focus on actions, on the quality of community life, on the quality of the lived experience of every individual. Still, her vision for neighbour-love goes beyond taking the initiative to meet immediate needs. Indeed, in her 1980 Christmas message she set out a comprehensive vision for neighbour-love that embraced every sphere of society from business to education, from the armed forces to health services, from politics to the arts. We love our neighbour by offering our gifts and talents to them in selfless service. Importantly, she closed that section of the message with these words:

> 'To all of you on this Christmas Day, whatever your conditions of work and life, easy or difficult; whether you feel that you are achieving something or whether you feel frustrated; I want to say a word of thanks. And I include all those who don't realise that they deserve thanks and are content that what

they do is unseen and unrewarded. The very act of living a decent and upright life is in itself a positive factor in maintaining civilised standards.'

It is as if the Queen had internalised the truth of Colossians 3:17 and 3:23-24. Yes, we can 'do whatever we do for God' whoever we are: slave or free, rich or poor, British-born or new immigrant.

Furthermore, it is not only that anyone can contribute and anything can be done for God, but that anything can be done with *love*:

'...billions of people now follow his [Christ's] teaching and find in him the guiding light for their lives. I am one of them because Christ's example helps me see the value of doing small things with great love, whoever does them and whatever they themselves believe.' (2016)

In sum, one of the reasons the Queen follows Christ is because he so clearly and consistently practices what he preaches. In him, word and deed match perfectly. He calls us to do the same. And so, in her speeches to the nation, the Queen echoes his call, encouraging every person to see that they have both a responsibility and an opportunity to contribute to the national good.

'Remember that good spreads outwards and every little does help. Mighty things from small beginnings grow as indeed they grew from the small child of Bethlehem.'

Elizabeth II
Christmas Address 1976

DO
GOOD
OPPOSE
EVIL

Inevitably, Elizabeth spends the majority of each Christmas message celebrating and summoning the good in the nation and the Commonwealth. But her addresses are often sharply attuned to national and global events – and alert to philosophical and attitudinal threats to the realisation of her vision. When Telstar, the first communications satellite, was launched in 1962 and Western people were increasingly vaunting technology as the solution to the woes of humankind, she was crystal clear about its limitations:

> *'The wise men of old followed a star; modern man has built one. But unless the message of this new star is the same as theirs our wisdom will count for nought.'*

Similarly, long before appeals to a particular definition of 'tolerance' threatened to limit respectful debate, she laid out a compelling framework for true tolerance and a sharp critique of lazy thinking:

> *'I speak of a tolerance that is not indifference, but is rather a willingness to recognise the possibility of right in others; of a comradeship that is not just a sentimental journey of good days past, but the certainty that the tried and staunch friends of yesterday are still in truth the same people today; of a love that can rise above anger and is ready to forgive...*

> *'The trouble is caused by unthinking people who carelessly throw away ageless ideals, as if they were old and outworn machinery. They would have religion thrown aside, morality in personal and public life made meaningless, honesty counted as foolishness and self-interest set up in place of self-restraint.'*

Those words sound remarkably pertinent today. They were written in 1957.

Elsewhere, she critiqued materialism (1968), spoke out on disability (1981) and child poverty (1979), called for greater equality and opportunity for women worldwide as early as 1966, and highlighted the need to care for the planet way back in 1989, specifically tying it to the command to love one's neighbour. In sum, the Queen is much more radical than we might suppose. The measured pace and emotional reserve of her delivery conceals the forthrightness of some of her statements.

There was, however, never any pretence that neighbourliness is easy. She is aware of the pressures and distractions that can lead us away from meeting our responsibilities and is grateful particularly for those who persevere despite the acuteness of their own challenges. She is aware too that 'love one another as I have loved you' is not a guru's suggestion, but a divine command. As she put it, 'It sounds so simple, yet it proves so hard to obey' (1995). And obedience to God is important to her because she is conscious of 'my own accountability before God' (2000).

And this perhaps explains the character qualities that she repeatedly affirms – resilience, determination, courage, perseverance in the face of rejection. All qualities she finds in Christ.

Given the Queen's belief in every person's capacity to contribute, it's not surprising that she does not pick out many individuals for personal praise in her Christmas messages – Mother Teresa and Nelson Mandela are exceptions. But when she does, it is for specific reasons: Mother Teresa for her understanding that love can be shown in the small things (2016); Nelson Mandela for his leadership in the work of forgiveness and reconciliation:

'It is time to recognise that in the end we all depend upon each other and that we are therefore responsible for each other.'

Elizabeth II
Christmas Address 1974

> 'The most gracious of men has shown us all how to accept the facts of the past without bitterness, how to see new opportunities as more important than old disputes and how to look forward with courage and optimism.' (1995)

Interestingly, this very reticence about citing individuals makes the one occasion when she dedicated a significant part of her Christmas address to one individual all the more remarkable

In 1992, Windsor Castle, now the Queen's main residence, was devastated by a fire. In the same year, three of her children's marriages were damaged beyond repair. She called it her *annus horribilis* (Latin for 'terrible year') – and in the midst of it, she found perspective in the life and work of Leonard Cheshire.

Cheshire was a former bomber pilot. He had received the Victoria Cross – not, as normally, for a single instance of extraordinary valour in the face of the enemy, but, as happens very rarely, for gallantry over the course of his entire operational career. He had converted to Catholicism in 1948 and founded what is now known as Leonard Cheshire Disability, a charity that makes a huge contribution to the wellbeing of disabled people around the world. His contributions were so admired that in 2002, he was voted number 31 in the BBC's list of the 100 Greatest Britons. In 1992, in her *annus horribilis*, Cheshire visited the Queen while in the terminal stage of motor neurone disease. In her Christmas address, she commended his selfless focus on making life better for others and highlighted the source of his inspiration:

> '*I have seen at first hand the remarkable results of his, and his wife [Sue Ryder]'s determination to put Christ's teaching to practical effect.*'

Perhaps even more telling is how she testifies to Christ's contribution to her own capacity to serve and his availability to others:

> '*There is no magic formula that will transform sorrow into happiness, intolerance into compassion or war into peace, but inspiration can change human behaviour. Those like Leonard Cheshire who devote their lives to others have that inspiration, and they know and we know where to look for help in finding it. That help can be readily given if we only have the faith to ask.*'

Here, then, we see that the servant life is not something Elizabeth can live in her own strength. For her, Christ is more than an example to follow, or a teacher who points the way, he is the source of power to live out what he calls his people to do. Indeed, the word 'readily' reveals a picture of a God who is eager to bless, who wants to help, a reality so often revealed in the Bible:

'If you then, though you are evil, know how to give good gifts to your children, how much more will your Father in heaven give the Holy Spirit to those who ask him!' (Luke 11:13)

'Christ not only revealed to us the truth in his teachings. He lived by what he believed and gave us the strength to try to do the same – and, finally, on the cross, he showed the supreme example of physical and moral courage.'

Elizabeth II
Christmas Address 1981

A
VISION
FOR THE
COMMONWEALTH

Just as the Queen's vision for the United Kingdom is rooted in biblical values, so too is her vision for the Commonwealth.

When she came to the throne, the Commonwealth consisted of eight nations. Today, 54 nations and territories, almost all former colonies, are members. How do you turn nations that your own country has conquered, ruled, and exploited for decades into friends?

In our deeply fractured world, how has it happened that 54 nations from five continents, with very different cultures and diverse religious majorities, should choose to meet regularly – not out of military expediency or vital economic self-interest, but out of a commitment to a shared vision for a different kind of world?

The short answer is: through the determination, warmth, and relational skills of the Queen. In her 1953 Christmas address, she said:

> 'The Commonwealth bears no resemblance to the empires of the past. It is an entirely new conception built on the highest qualities of the spirit of man: friendship, loyalty, and the desire for freedom and peace. To that new conception of an equal partnership of nations and races I shall give myself heart and soul every day of my life.'

It was another promise she would keep. At the Silver Jubilee, she said that she had witnessed:

> 'From a unique position ... the last great phase of the transformation of the Empire into Commonwealth and the transformation of the Crown from an emblem of dominion into a symbol of free and voluntary association. In all history, this has no precedent.'

It is a remarkable achievement. Reconciliation in action. Where might the Queen have got such a vision?

It is an idea that belongs to neither the left nor the right. It is rooted in the Queen's understanding of God's concern for all human beings, of the example

Christmas speeches
where the Queen
speaks about peace.

1950s   ●●●●●○●○●
1960s   ●●○●○●●●●○
1970s   ○●●○○○●●○○
1980s   ●○●●●●●●○○
1990s   ○○●●●●●●○○
2000s   ●●○●●●●●●●
2010s   ●○●○●●○●●●
2020s   ●○

of 'the child who was born at Christmas with a love that came to embrace the whole world' (1995). And it is underpinned by the Queen's biblical understanding of the equality of all human beings under God, and of the calling of all Christians to seek to love all people.

Beyond that, the possibility of peace among all nations comes straight out of the biblical promise of a day when the tanks will be turned into tractors, or, as Isaiah 2:4 puts it, 'swords into ploughshares'. A day when nation will not fight against nation, when peace will reign across the globe. Of course, such a vision will only be fully realised when Christ returns and creation is renewed, but that did not stop the Queen working to create a context in which understanding could grow, cooperation flourish, and inequalities be addressed.

It is a measure of the Commonwealth's value that even when Pakistan left because the other members recognised Bangladesh, they felt the association was important enough to re-join some 17 years later. And in 2021, when Barbados became a republic rather than a constitutional monarchy under the Queen, it stayed a member of the Commonwealth. The proud island nation invited Prince Charles to make a speech on Elizabeth's behalf, in which he reaffirmed her vision:

'I was so deeply touched that you should have invited me to return to Barbados and to join you, on behalf of The Queen... As your constitutional status changes, it was important to me that I should join you to reaffirm those things which do not change. For example, the close and trusted partnership between Barbados and the United Kingdom as vital members of the Commonwealth; our common determination to defend the values we both cherish and to pursue the goals we share; and the myriad connections between the people of our countries – through which flow admiration and affection, co-operation and opportunity – strengthening and enriching us all.'

'The gift I would most value next year is that reconciliation should be found wherever it is needed. A reconciliation which would bring peace and security to families and neighbours at present suffering and torn apart.'

Elizabeth ll
Christmas Address 1976

CHURCH
AND
WITNESS

The Queen is the head of the Church of England, and a regular worshipper who extols the joy of corporate worship and the value of prayer. Nevertheless, in her Christmas addresses she never explicitly encourages anyone to go to church. But she does occasionally go out of her way to affirm followers of Christ. For example, in 1993, she again explored the theme of service, particularly in relation to those who contribute unobtrusively. To encourage them, she said:

> 'I am always moved by those words in St John's Gospel which we hear on Christmas Day – "He was in the world, and the world was made by him, and the world knew him not..." We have only to listen to

the news to know the truth of that. But the Gospel goes on – "But as many as received him, to them gave he power to become the sons of God".

'For all the inhumanity around us, let us be grateful for those who have received him and who go about quietly doing their work and his will without thought of reward or recognition. They know that there is an eternal truth of much greater significance than our own triumphs and tragedies, and it is embodied by the Child in the Manger. That is their message of hope.'

It is a direct affirmation of Christians – for those with ears to hear – delivered in a way that avoids the label and minimises the barriers to exploration and belief for those who aren't Christians. At the same time, in her commendation of *Songs of Praise* on its 60th anniversary in 2021, we can see that she appreciates the difference between church attendance and discipleship:

'...the programme has shown Christianity as a living *faith not only through hymns and worship songs, but also by featuring the many people who have put their faith at the centre of their lives.'* (Emphasis mine.)

Faith in Christ is not a peripheral pursuit or a leisure-time bolt-on, but something 'living' that should shape our whole lives. We are not just saved by faith. We live by it (2 Corinthians 5:7).

'He knew rejection, hardship and persecution: and yet it is Jesus Christ's generous love and example which has inspired me through good times and bad.'

Elizabeth II
Christmas Address 2015

Nevertheless, the Queen never specifically says that Jesus is 'the only way to the Father'. In the early decades, she rarely mentioned the words 'Jesus' or 'Christ' specifically. That began to change in the 90s, and by the 2000s she not only said 'Jesus', 'Christ', or both in most of her addresses, she spoke much more explicitly about her personal commitment. In 16 of the 21 addresses between 2000 and 2021, she used the first person singular or the inclusive 'we' to refer to her faith – 'my prayer' (2012), 'inspired me' (2017), 'I believe' (2018). Her overall approach became testimonial, sharing her deep personal gratitude for Christ and the transformative difference he makes in her life.

Some might prefer her to be clearer about Jesus as the only one through whom we can be saved (Acts 4:12), though few would quibble with the heartfelt conclusion to her 2011 address:

> 'It is my prayer that on this Christmas day we might all find room in our lives for the message of the angels and for the love of God through Christ our Lord.'

Others would say that her communication strategy is well suited to TV and to the times we're in. Personal story is powerful and attractive. As one young evangelist put it, 'She has maintained a long-term, winsome, clear and unapologetic witness to Jesus, without alienating people of other faiths or none.'

Indeed, one of the reasons she is so admired by
people of other faiths is precisely because she is
a person of sincere faith herself and understands
the role that living faith plays in people's lives. As
head of the Church of England, she sees that it 'has
a duty to protect the free practice of all faiths in
this country' (Lambeth Palace, 2012). Again, this is
rooted in Christ's example:

> 'For me, the life of Jesus Christ, the Prince of Peace,
> whose birth we celebrate today, is an inspiration and
> an anchor in my life. A role-model of reconciliation
> and forgiveness, he stretched out his hands in love,
> acceptance, and healing. Christ's example has
> taught me to seek to respect and value all people of
> whatever faith or none.' (2014)

Indeed, her focus is very much on Jesus. Almost
all the biblical quotations she uses are from the
Gospels and are either about Jesus or spoken by
him. It's clear that her confidence lies in him, and
in the efficacy of his ways. See, for example, how
gently, humbly, honestly, and robustly she testifies
to that: 'It is not always easy to accept his teaching,
but I have no doubt that the New Year will be all
the better if we do but try' (2002).

That said, the Queen does not commend Jesus
merely as a teacher example, and source of
strength, but something more too:

> 'Although we are capable of great acts of kindness,

*history teaches us that we sometimes need saving
from ourselves – from our recklessness or our greed.
God sent into the world a unique person – neither
a philosopher nor a general (important though they
are) – but a Saviour, with the power to forgive.*

*'Forgiveness lies at the heart of the Christian faith. It
can heal broken families, it can restore friendships,
and it can reconcile divided communities. It is in
forgiveness that we feel the power of God's love.'*
(2011)

We need 'saving from ourselves'. She's including
herself in that. Indeed, there is no sense of moral
superiority or judgementalism in her summons
to the good or her naming of the human need for
forgiveness. Rather, she is clear about her own
limitations and need for help.

*'I know just how much I rely on my faith to guide me
through the good times and the bad. Each day is a
new beginning. I know that the only way to live my
life is to try to do what is right, to take the long view,
to give of my best in all that the day brings, and to
put my trust in God!'* (2002)

Just in those words you can see the biblical roots
that fuel her life: seeking wisdom from above
(James 1:5), not leaning on her own understanding
(Proverbs 3:5-6), depending on God in the good
times (Deuteronomy 6:10-12) as well as the bad
(Psalm 10:14), recognising each day as a new

beginning (Lamentations 3:23), seeking to do the right thing (Matthew 6:33), avoiding short-termism (Philippians 1:6), giving her best in 'all' (Ephesians 5:15-17). And all of that then summed up in that elemental, worshipful confession of her trust in God, that she draws strength 'from the message of hope in the Christian gospel.'

Of course, there is so much we don't know about the Queen's faith, but what we can see is this: it's rich, it's alive, it's constant, it's prayerful, it's biblical, and it's Christ-centred. It's shaped her imagination and it's enabled her to model gracious excellence in arguably the most public role in the world for over 70 years. And that faith, that living trust in Christ, has impelled her to give the credit to the Saviour whose servant heart and servant example she has sought to emulate in everything she does.

Praise God indeed.

✝

Quotations and references taken from Elizabeth II's speeches:

Speech by the Queen on Her 21st Birthday
21 April 1947

Silver Jubilee Speech in the Guildhall
6 June 1977

Address at Lambeth Palace
15 February 2012

Commendation of *Songs of Praise*
3 October 2021

And the Queen's Christmas addresses in these years:

1950s   ○●●○●●○○

1960s   ●○●○○○●○○○

1970s   ●○●●○○●○●○

1980s   ○●○○●○○○○●

1990s   ●○●●○●○○○○

2000s   ●○●○○○●○○●

2010s   ○●●●●●●●●○

2020s   ○○

About Mark Greene

Ex-adman, ex-Bible College Vice-Principal, Mark is LICC's Mission Champion. His focus is on empowering God's people to be fruitful for Christ in their Monday to Saturday lives. His books include the million-copy selling *The Servant Queen and the King She Serves* (with Catherine Butcher), *Thank God it's Monday: Ministry in the Workplace,* and *Fruitfulness on the Frontline*.

About LICC

The Queen's faith makes a noticeable difference to her everyday life. But how does trusting Jesus change the way you might work, shop, relate to friends, watch a movie, comment online, help people in need? Find out more about how The London Institute for Contemporary Christianity empowers individuals and churches for whole-life discipleship through resources, research, teaching, and training at **licc.org.uk**

About Bible Society

Working in over 200 countries, Bible Society is on a mission to make the Bible available and understood around the world. This is because we believe that when people engage with the Scriptures lives can be changed, for good. HM The Queen is the Patron of Bible Society. Find out more about Bible Society's work at **biblesociety.org.uk**